'TEENAGE MATTERS'

Copyright © 2016 Olabode Desire Omogbehin

First published in February 2016 by
LIFEBOOKS DESIRE PUBLISHING COMPANY

This is a book project by
DIVINE PROVIDENCE SUPPORT FOUNDATION
Request for information on this book
should be addressed to
Desire Omogbehin
Email – info@desireola.com
bodeduet@yahoo.com

ACKNOWLEDGEMENT

I am full of appreciation to God for blessing me with incredible individuals who have contributed to my life and sharpened my destiny in Christ. I cannot mention all the names here for the purpose of space and time. However, I will not fail to mention a few such individuals who have impacted my life directly especially for this book.

I acknowledge the invaluable love of Pastor Tunde Netufo, Pastor Afilaka, Pastor Awoyale, and Pastor Tope Smart all from The Redeem Christian Church of God. You all have been instrumental to what I am today. Also, thank you, Mr. McRoberts, of 3rd-Degree Photography, Jos.

Never forgetting Dr. Bayo Kolade for his support through-out the process of book writing and publishing.

Special thanks to my wife Abisola and our lovely Children. Thank you for inspiring me and giving towards the success of this book project.

Thank you for believing in me and for giving me the chance to embark on this project.

To all my mentors, friends, colleagues, seniors, staff, associates, and any other person I have been privileged to work with and learn from; thank you for never giving up on me.

I also want to thank many academicians, scientists, researchers, teacher, and educationist out there who put out great contents and contribute positively to the entire benefit of mankind and humanity.

DEDICATION

This book is dedicated to God Almighty.

I also want to dedicate this book to all focused teenagers and youths around the world.

Teenage Matters

INTRODUCTION

Ever since the discovery, spread and use of the internet, and social media across the world, a lot of things have changed rapidly. If you ask me, I'd tell you that there has been a significant and positive impact as a result of this development. However, I can also tell you without mincing words the downsides to it as well which leaves me to say trouble looms ahead.

I remember clearly when I was in high school; I knew some notorious friends who got involved in all manner of immoral and immodest acts. Those days, drugs and pornography were some of the acts they did secretly. As at then, they probably would have to go steal the tapes from adults or find a way of buying from a seller who doesn't care about the consequences or implications. The fact was that, whether they succeeded in stealing or buying it, the whole process was not easy at all. However, a few years after, having access to these illicit materials became easier because many vendors and stores now display them openly for innocent shoppers. In this present age, you don't even need to buy any more; such materials are now everywhere showing on our screens and gadgets. Things have changed drastically and rapidly; it is no longer business as usual for us. One way or the other, you are faced with explicit scenes and acts. Now, we have many sexual perverts and pedophiles who do not think of their consequences even before the acts. Unfortunately, our children, teenagers, and youths are at the receiving end. And, if nothing is done to counter check this 'risk', things may get out of hand before we know it. Don't get me wrong, it is not as if there weren't illicit acts right from time past, my main point is that things have really gotten out of hand and we must collectively act fast before it blows right on our faces. This is one of the reasons why this book was written in a bid to reach out to many teenagers and youths across the globe.

Present-day exposure

One of my female friends once shared her personal story with me. She is way older than I am; her kids are already grown to become teenagers. Now, she said her mother is of the opinion that she is not training her kids well enough. Many times, she looked at her unpleasantly and then said things like, "look at what you allow your kids do, this was not how we raised you"; or how could you allow your kids wear that, drink that, talk like that, this wasn't like this before". Now each time she spoke like, it made my friend look like she is not a good mother to her children or that she is not doing well enough at raising her kids. But then, she summoned courage and told her mom one day " Grandma, I am trying my best, things are not just the same again as they were when you were raising me and my siblings". However, it was still a source of concern to her and many times, she had to voice out to someone like me, asking what else she probably should do differently to help her children. Well, some of us had given her some good tips which seem to be working. But the fact remains to be that truly, Grandma has not yet realized the present-day challenges, harmful exposures, and distractions that have taken over teens/youths of this generation.

Peer pressure

There is nothing that easily changes the focus, and goal of any teenager other than peer pressure. And almost everyone likes to associate with other people and as such end up having lifestyles that replicate after each other. It is not a bad thing to have friends or relate with other people. As a matter of fact, you need the help of others to actualize your dream fast enough.

Surely, moving with bad company, association, group, friends, is what is bad. The people we relate with will determine what becomes of our lives. To a large extent, the people we relate with dictate how we live our lives including our attitudes and behavior. They dictate what we wear, what we eat, what we listen to, watch, go and many more. This is the pressure we receive from them as a result of associating with their peer group. Combating or dealing with these pressures is not always easy to do; therefore, it is important to choose or pick the kind of friends we move or relate with. It is not a crime if you decide to pick or select your own friends or company. Nevertheless, it can be a crime if you allow your friends to pick or determine your lifestyle.

This book will help and guide you in knowing the importance of selecting your own friends and company.

Combating bad habits

A friend once told me that anything you do consistently for 21 times/days rotational, automatically becomes a habit. Habits don't just happen suddenly. They usually start with a step, two steps, three trials and more, before it eventually becomes permanent (habit). For you to live a purposeful life; and to achieve your dreams/goals in life, you must do away with bad habits. A drug addict didn't just become one suddenly; he/she probably started playing with putting smokes on papers at home; taking one shot; taking few drugs to sleep or get high and then trying to do more and more. The truth is that whatever bad thing you have a passion for, and you eventually do may create a sensation or feeling that soothes you just for a while, which you may never get out of easily except with help from those around you who truly care. Our body systems are built in such a way that it tries to acclimatize with whatever it is fed with consistently. Therefore, for instance, if you love to take a bottle of alcoholic drink, a time comes when you want to take two because your body system automatically works to contain the effect of that one bottle. You will then find out that you want to take more and more till you are totally alcoholic. The best antidote/remedy to bad habit is never to go near or try it. Once you try it, you may find it very difficult to stop. I have a line I like to repeat to youths I have the opportunity to speak with- *"NO TRIAL, NO ADDICTIONS."*

A young teenager once asked me an intelligent question. He wanted to know if virgins too do have sexual urges like non-virgins. My answer was simple, and it was that you rarely have an urge or feelings of what you have never tasted. As an individual, you rarely would have an urge to taste Apples once you have never tasted or seen one before. You rarely would have an urge to eat a specific food if you have never tasted or seen it before. But the day you try it out, or the day you see it prepared, or the day you are told about it; you may 'desire' or 'wish' to taste it. At that point, it may be called a mere fantasy; it is not called an urge. It becomes an urge after you have tasted it and you want to have more. The urge can be said to be that feeling that accompanies dissatisfaction which is usually after a 'taste' or an 'encounter'.

It is an inclination to want more of something after tasting them. Therefore, there is no way a virgin could have sexual urge if he/she has never been 'exposed' to sexual materials or engaged in close sexual acts.

Bad habits are like viruses that are very easy to stick to you and spread rapidly over a period. But I will say again that the best approach to deal with bad habits is to ensure that you don't even go near or try anything called bad habits. And for you not to engage in such acts, self-discipline and understanding are very important for you to possess.

And for whoever has gotten involved with any form of a bad habit and wants to get out of it, there is a healing process if you are willing. Please take note that there has to be the 'willingness' from you first of all. No willingness, No healing.

Therefore, for every teenager or youth who wants to make a positive mark in life; this is the right book for you.

Sit back, relax, enjoy, and learn new things about yourself and others.

CHAPTER ONE

SEXUALITY

Everyone's sexuality is different, and it's not necessarily as simple as 'gay' (homosexual) or 'straight' (heterosexual) anymore. When we talk about sexuality, many individuals across the world are attracted to people of the same sex, while others may have affection to a diversity of individuals regardless of the gender or sexual preference as it may apply. Some gay, lesbian or bisexual people say, that from an early age that they "felt different" and had crushes on best friends, or people of the same sex, meaning they could only associate these feelings with being gay or bisexual later as they grow.

Every day of our lives, we talk about sex, read about it, see things that are related to it and even hear other people discuss this same subject matter. As a matter of fact, it has come to become a part of us continuously affecting us consciously or unconsciously. But wait a minute, a lot of what we read, see, and hear about sex and sexuality are not all that accurate, and they are sometimes confusing, misleading or even harmful to us. However, if only one has a basic understanding of sex and sexuality, it can help us sort out myths from facts while also helping us make good decisions about our general sexual health. This is true because sexuality affects who we are including how we also express ourselves. The way people see their sexuality differ from one person to another. At this point, I am not going to rule out one in favor of another. The truth is that no one determined what their sexuality will be. While some people may have control over their sexuality, some other people do not have such control.

Some people are very sexual, while others experience no feelings or interest in sexual attraction at all (asexual). If we search deep down in ourselves, we can easily tell which category we belong to.

Many people don't discover their sexual attractions until much later into adulthood which leaves ones with some form of confusion too. Truly, knowing your sexuality can be confusing. So, don't worry if you aren't sure where you belong yet. At an early age is the best time to figure out what works for you; and those strong feelings in you including the exploration are parts of it. Surely, a time comes when you will be able to find out if you are drawn mostly to men or to women or even to both or to neither; at that point in time, you will certainly know your sexuality.

In fact, to an extent, we will also be able to tell which category our friends belong judging from how they react or respond to sexually related things. More so, please note that your sexuality may as well be influenced by your own family, culture, religion, media, friends, and experiences you go through in life. No matter how important sexuality is to you, we all have thoughts, desires, attractions, and values that are unique from one another. Nevertheless, for the purpose of a proper understanding, I will like to say that sexuality is about much more than just 'sex'.

It also includes the following which are:

Your body, including your sexual and reproductive anatomy and body image i.e. how you feel about your body.

Your biological sex - male, female, and mixed-sex (hermaphrodite) which is usually rare and regarded as exceptional.

Your gender — being a girl, boy, woman, or man. Nowadays, we also have the transgendered people which is regarded as a self-choice.

Gender identity - talks about how you choose to express your gender. What sex do you want people to know you with?

Your sexual orientation – could refer to who you are sexually and/or romantically attracted to. It could also mean your thoughts, values, attitudes, sexual fantasies, and preferences.

Your sexual behaviors and beliefs - which could include abstinence, sexual positions, polygamy (polygyny or polyandry), or keeping more than one partner, celibacy, and any other form of sexual addictions.

In general, it is a good thing for teenagers and youths to ask questions about sex and sexuality. There is a general consciousness that the more you know about a thing, the less confused you become. In my home country, there is an adage that says "he who asks for the road direction can never get lost on the way." Therefore, take charge of yourself, take charge of your sexuality before it takes charge of you.

TYPES OF SEXUALITY

Talking about identity, there are a few categories and characteristics associated with it.

Technically speaking, I will say that your sexuality is not necessarily defined by who you have sex with, but about how you feel and how you choose to identify yourself. Knowing where you belong is the first step to knowing your sexuality as well as understanding yourself (body). You must know where you belong so that you can easily deal with your body peradventure you have very rare or exceptional sexuality.

I cannot condemn anyone for their sexuality outrightly but having gone far and wide in study and research across the globe; it has become very clear that the rightest sexuality generally acceptable is Heterosexuality. All other types of sexuality have been regarded as rare and exceptional cases. Listed below are the basic types of sexuality.

Straight (Heterosexual) - they are attracted to people of the opposite sex or gender. This is the ideal kind of sexuality as ordained by God.

Homo-sexual (Gay) is a general term used for people who have affection toward individuals of the same gender or sex. It is a commonly used term for the male gender.

Lesbian (Homosexual) –they are attracted to people of the same sex or gender. It is a commonly used term for the female.

Mixed-sex (Bisexual) - attracted to both men and women. Some people use terms like pan or pansexual to say they are attracted to rather different kinds of people, regardless of their gender.

Asexual – are those people who are not interested or sexually attracted to anyone. This is a rare type of sexuality and it is said to be that about 1% of the world population is in this category.

Although, it is possible to have an individual from other types of sexuality becoming asexual. This could be related to a bitter experience that could have happened to them, or an accident or maybe just as a result of a hormonal imbalance.

CHAPTER TWO
HUMAN SEXUALITY

Human sexuality in this context can be said to be the capacity of humans to have 'erotic' experiences and responses. An individual's orientation when it comes to sex can affect how they get attracted to another individual.

Sexuality in humans can be expressed, and experienced in many ways which can include but not limited to beliefs, thoughts, practices, desires, values, ideas, behaviors, fantasies, and attitudes.

These expressions can be manifested in different ways socially, physically, legally, materially, financially, emotionally, politically, philosophically, morally, biologically and spiritually. Many people cannot explain why they are attracted to a particular gender other than the fact they get deep feelings or arousal for the individual.

Expressions done through emotional and physical means are related to sexuality expressed through physical bonds and the manifestation of care and love, or through profound feelings by those individuals involved. The category of people who are sexually attracted to an individual based on strong emotions are called "Demisexual."

More-so, expressions done through physical and biological means are concerned with human reproductive functions and sexual response cycle as found in different individuals and even in different species. At this stage, we would talk about the XY-male category and the XX-female category of chromosomes. Study also shows that the higher the chromosomes you have among these two would likely determine your sexual behavior. This is the reason why some scientists concluded that some gender choice has a purely hormonal imbalance. Sexual activity is part of human need and living and therefore requires a connection (affection), drive (energy), and pleasure (intimacy).

Spirituality in this sense refers to personal beliefs and norms of a community-backed up by a supreme being, while the social means refer to the impact of the society on an individual's choice of sexuality.

Legally and moral talks about the kind of sexuality that deemed right and acceptable by the laws binding that community, city, or country. In this case, an opposite behavior, expression, or attitude could be punishable by the law.

SEXUAL ACTIVITY

This results in erotic love, intimate friendship, human mating, including procreation. A basic fact has emerged showing that interest in sexual activity typically increases when an individual reaches puberty or when one is fully aware of their sexuality. Although, opinions differ on the origin of an individual's sexual orientation and their sexual behavior. Some argue that sexuality is determined by genetics while some believe it is molded by the environment, and others argue that both factors interact to form the individual's sexual orientation. This pertains to nature versus nurture debate. While the genetic nature believes that the features of an individual regardless of gender corresponds to their inheritance or genes, the environmental factor is believed that the features of an individual will continuously change throughout their lifetime of nurturing and development. Whichever way, the sexual activity of anyone is basically determined deeply by how exposed they are to the generic word sex.

SEXUAL ATTRACTION

Sexual attraction can be said to be a form of drawing attention based on sexual desire or the quality of arousing such interest. By defining an individual's sexual appeal or attractiveness, we refer to the person's ability to call the erotic or sexual attention of the other person. Attractiveness is very personal and is based on mate choice or physical qualities. It is rather amazing and shocking to know what people are attracted to in the other person. Attractions may come from different preferences from other people such as the lifestyle of the other individual, their taste of fashion, as well as the perfume they wear, the color of the skin, or the hairstyle among others. For example, a gay or lesbian person would typically find a person of the same sex to be more attractive than one of the other sexes while a bisexual person would find either sex to be attractive. Asexuality, on the other hand, refers to those who do not experience sexual attraction for either sex, although they might have some romantic attraction which can also be in the categories of biromantic, homo, or heteroromantic.

SEXUALITY AND RELIGION

Based on different religions as we might have seen across the world, sexual behaviors are seen in different ways and perspectives.

In others, it is treated as primarily physical. Some religions hold that sexual behavior is only spiritual within certain kinds of relationships, when used for specific purposes, or when incorporated into religious ritual. For some of the religions across the world, there could be not much difference in the spiritual and physical aspects of sexuality. Although, many religions believe human sexuality will compliment the gap between the spiritual and the physical.

Many religious conservatives, especially those of Christianity and Islam in particular, tend to view sexuality as a choice rather than a natural phenomenon. Therefore, sexuality such as bisexuality, homosexuality, or heterosexuality are all a function of what an individual chose to become. These conservatives tend to promote celibacy for gay people instead and may also tend to believe that sexuality can be changed through conversion therapy or prayers to become an ex-gay. They may also see homosexuality as a form of mental illness, something that ought to be criminalized, an immoral abomination, caused by ineffective parenting, while also viewing same-sex marriage as a threat to the society. Although, some religions are now becoming neutral to what used to criminalize, and now tag it legally and morally acceptable. Therefore, these religions would not relate some sexuality to mental illness influenced by genetics, bad parenting, or the environment.

According to Judaism, sex is between a man and a woman bounded in marriage and therefore, must be held sacred and enjoyed with celibacy being considered sinful. According to the Catholics, their doctrine teaches that sexuality is worthy and noble which must, however, be used according to the natural biblical law. Therefore, the only acceptable form of sexual activity is the one between a man and a woman without any asunder.

Also, when it comes to intercourse, any sexual pleasure that is not for the possibility of conception is considered sinful and immoral. The Roman Catholic Church has condemned self-pleasure (masturbation), the use of pills, and contraceptives, and homosexualism. Also, they have supported abstinence and we have seen a group of individuals called priests and nuns emerging from Catholicism. Priests and nuns are allowed to marry now once they are laicized (no more religious vows).

Also, in Islam, sexual desire is considered a natural urge that should not be suppressed, although the concept of free sex is not accepted; and these urges should be fulfilled responsibly. The term used for marriage within the Quran is

'Nikah', which is an Arabic word and literally means sexual intercourse. Although Islamic sexuality is restrained through Islamic sexual jurisprudence, it emphasizes sexual pleasure within marriage. Also, in Islam, it is acceptable for a man to have more than one wife, but he must take care of those wives physically, mentally, emotionally, financially, and spiritually at the same measure. Muslims believe that sexual intercourse is an act of worship that fulfills emotional and physical needs and that producing children is one way in which humans can contribute to God's creation. Also, Islam discourages celibacy once an individual is married.

Furthermore, homosexuality in Islam is strictly forbidden with many Islamic scholars suggesting that those who practice such acts ought to be put to death. However, many Islamic scholars, on the other hand, suggested that Islam has an open approach to sex as far as it is done within the marriage and is free is of adultery, lewdness, and fornication. For many Muslims, sex with reference to the Quran indicates that a non-approval of anal intercourse. Also, an Islamic home bounded by Nikah marital contract believes that a husband and his wife(s) should enjoy and even indulge, within the privacy of their marital home.

Moreover, Hinduism as a religion, emphasizes that sex is only appropriate between husband and wife, in which satisfying sexual urges through sexual pleasure is an important duty of marriage. Any sex before marriage is considered to interfere with intellectual development, especially between birth and the age of 25; and therefore, encouraged to be avoided or abstained.

CHAPTER THREE

EARLY SEX

The Adolescent stage which is basically the period between 12 and 17 years of age, is a crucial phase in the development of any individual and it is also the period in which one's sexuality is discovered, along with the questions related to it. It is a period when teenagers begin to consider what sexual behavior could be pleasurable, morally acceptable and appropriate for their age. Although it has been proven statistically, that sexual activity during early adolescence can be harmful in both psychological and physical terms. However, the phenomenon of precocious sexual activity shows how sex is present in the lives of adolescents even before they are ready for the consequences it can have. There is more harm done than good when we elucidate this subject matter of early sex.

EFFECTS OF EARLY SEX

Based on what I have read personally, results, and findings of different articles show that young boys who get exposed to sexually explicit materials would three-times likely engage in sexual acts than non-exposed boys two-years after exposure.

The same goes for young girls who might experience early inappropriate exposure to sexual content. They are twice likely to engage in sexual acts or intercourse a few years after such exposure. The research also showed that teenagers who listen to immoral and degrading musical contents are more likely to engage in sexual acts than those who had no or little exposure.

Below are some of the negative effects of early sex:

High-Risk Sex

Similar to what has been explained in the paragraphs above, there is a high-risk sexual violence and involvement with children who have been exposed to sexual or adult contents. According to different studies and research, children within the ages of 11 and 13 who have sex at that stage are likely to become very promiscuous, engage in random and frequent intercourse with multiple partners. Exposures could be from the television, online, magazines, peer groups, or associations which could leave an indelible memory or impact in the lives of the teenager forever. This could even lead to teenagers wanting to try out adventurous sex that can be deadly.

I remember a story of two teenagers dating, got exposed to sex too early in their lives, and in the course of their relationship decided to explore their sexual fantasies at a balcony of a very tall building. They came across a hotel that suited their plans, booked the room on the last floor; got themselves drunk with so much alcohol, and started having sex right there at the balcony. Unfortunately for them, the girl tripped on the stool she was standing on, and just before anyone could know what was happening, they both fell from the balcony and landed on the ground floor. The police and paramedics arrived at the scene and found them dead naked and were able to conclude instantly the act that leads to their death.

Sex, Love, and Relationship Addictions

It is not to say that all mental health disorder is as a result of early exposure to sexual content. Also, several children who are exposed to sexual materials will suffer from mental health disorders. However, pornography has been found to be a high-risk factor for sexual addictions and other intimacy disorders. In one study of 832 sex addicts, 91 percent of men and 79 percent of women reported that pornography was a factor in their addiction. With the widespread availability of explicit material on the Internet nowadays, these problems are becoming more prevalent and are surfacing even for the younger ages.

Sexual Violence

A teenager who has been exposed to explicit and provocative sexual materials are a very early stage will soon become a victim of sexual prey or violator. Naturally, humans are influenced by what they see or hear, thus making people wanting to act out what they see. And if as a child or a teenager, and all you see are depictions of hate, rape, drugs, humiliation, and torture, then, there could be the tendency to accept the abnormal as the norm. Many now wonder why our society is full of crime, it's not far from the fact that these individuals who act in an absurd manner already had their minds tampered at the very early stage of their lives. All of which are prevalent in our times and seasons.

Regrets and disappointments

Sex 'too early' can lead to regret and disappointment for many teenagers. Many girls end up regretting losing their virginity at an early age. A study carried out by researchers from the University of Western Australia (UWA) found out that teenage girls who lose their virginities when they are not ready often at an earlier age; are more likely to feel disappointed and also regret the experience entirely for the rest of their lives. By the way, I'd like to say here that the past cannot be changed but the future can be repaired. Let go of the past!

Unwanted Pregnancy

Having sex at a very early stage of one's life can lead to getting pregnant. It is not as if pregnancy is not a good thing, but early and unwanted pregnancy could disrupt your plans, make you lose your mind, your self-esteem, and could even ruin your career and dreams in life. After all, nobody on planet earth fell from the sky. Our parents took-in (got pregnant) for us to come to life. But then, having what you do not wish to come to life could be a disaster anyone can ever think or imagine. Every teenager I have met, always possess a big picture of what they intend to become in the later future. Unfortunately, some of them do not eventually achieve these great dreams because they gave in to early sex, got pregnant or possibly impregnated someone (the boys). Just imagine that you now have to be a father or a mother at a very early stage in life probably before or during high school when you are still under your parent's care or supervision.

This unwanted experience can be a nightmare that you do not wish to happen. Early sex can only lead to one thing which is teenage pregnancy. I will still elucidate further on this specific subject matter later in this book.

CHAPTER FOUR
EARLY SEX INFLUENCER

There has been a major concern for many people as to why teenagers are having sex at their young ages, certainly younger than previous generations despite knowing well enough that an early exposure to sexually provocative contents could lead to devastating repercussions such as STDs' or unwanted pregnancy. The reason for this is not far from the fact that teens are now more exposed to sexually related materials. Here, I want to quickly lay emphasis on some of those things that I know leads to young ones engaging in early sex.

The Television – Movies and Music and related videos

Among the major factors which can lead to adolescents prematurely addressing sexual relationships both from the family, political and pedagogic contexts, is the television. There are good, scientific reasons for thinking that television can contribute to precocious sexual activity. The truth is that sexual behavior is strongly influenced by culture and television is an integral part of adolescent culture.

The entertainment industry contributes to a larger percentage of harm rendered to many adolescents. Most of the music videos released nowadays are almost not children friendly. They are too explicit, promote promiscuity, and are extremely dangerous to watch. I seriously hope that the institution responsible for the release of these music videos get to screen them properly before approving their public viewing or listening. Based on different research and findings, movies and music are two powerful tools that have the potency to influence behaviors and attitudes. Therefore, teenagers who watch sexually driven movies or listen to profane songs that interpret drugs, rape, drunkenness, sexual violence, among others are likely to see the world and other individuals or genders differently.

We are not surprised that many men and women cannot get along easily when they finally settle down in a relationship. Reason being that so many ugly scenes and imaginations had influenced their thoughts and reasoning. Normal social values are becoming lost in the society, and hooliganism, drugs, and provocative nudity are being permitted all in the name of it is a free world and socialism.

According to different studies carried out in different parts of the world, adolescents watch up to an average of three hours of television a day. Another survey also confirmed that a higher percentage of most television contents including commercials have relatively explicit content referencing sex.

This high exposure which the young people have on sex can influence their ideas about cultural norms in television viewing; and can actually create an irrecoverable taste and deceits that sex is not sacrosanct and is the central part of daily life, while in reality, it is not. Exposure to social models provided by the television can also change opinions about the probable consequences which sexual activity brings with it. A sociological theory claims that adolescents who see people having casual sexual relations on television (or at the cinema) without negative consequences are more inclined to assume this behavior themselves. Although the television can also inhibit sexual relations by illustrating the risks especially the possibility of contracting a disease, infection or having unwanted pregnancies, encouraging abstinence or promoting safe sex. However, it rarely carries out this purpose on a large scale. As a result of this, Dr. Rebecca Collins's study, which was published in the September 2004 edition of the journal 'Pediatrics,' caused a lot of discussions as it demonstrated how the television can influence young people to have sexual relations at an early age.

Having picked up a signal from the American Academy of Pediatrics, which linked the phenomenon of sexual content in television programs (even if not explicit) to sex practiced during adolescence, Dr. Collins together with some other colleagues studied this rationale in scientific terms by examining a significant sample of 1,793 girls and boys who are within the ages of twelve and seventeen years. The sample size was selected from different areas and these young people were asked to talk about some of their television habits, and the answers given were compared with the results and findings of their analysis in order to obtain an assessment of sexual context. The results testified that 90% of adolescents who watch television programs that contain a lot of sexual content are twice as likely to start precocious sexual activity compared to those who watched less television. This piece of data is very significant if you think about the fact that so-called 'risky' programs, deemed so by the survey, were not only those which showed sexual acts but also those in which sex was purely spoken about.

This is not to say that teenagers should not watch television; it only means that watching television should always be reduced to the barest minimum or possibly used under parental guidance. It is important to encourage parents and schools to work towards a means of prevention that addresses sexual initiation during early adolescence so young people are aware of the risks they are exposing themselves to. Reducing the number of sexual contents in entertainment programs, reducing exposure of such content to adolescents, and 'offering explanations' about the possible negative consequences sexual activity on very young people could delay or prevent the onset of intercourse. Alternatively, parents of young people could help to minimize negative consequences by watching these programs with them and discussing the opinions they have concerning sex and the situations presented on television.

The Internet - Social Media

Ever since the wide use of the internet and social media, innocent teenagers have had exposure to millions of pages of materials and access to materials that are unfiltered, uncensored, including sexually immoral contents that are very harmful. With the massive number of materials and contents shared across the globe, this is almost uncontrollable. It is what I will personally tag online social pandemic.

In my opinion, the internet and social media are second to the television, in terms of damage done to our younger ones, when it comes to what they have access to. Even if young children can't understand sex or the role in relationships, the images they see leave a lasting impression on them. Teens are 85% more likely to engage in sexual activity after being exposed to some sexual content on social media. The reason for this is almost the same as when we read educative books and show educational movies to children in schools with the hope that they learn lessons from what they are seeing as well as learn from the characters. All these online contents that are unfiltered and uncensored expose our teenagers to dirtiness and a belief that sex is rather casual, without consequence, and an act that can be experimented anytime and anywhere.

Associations and peer group

Teenagers must be very careful with who they relate with or who they interact with. There is a general notion which says birds of the same feather flock together, and in addition to the popular opinion that says show me your friends, I will tell you who you are." I will add to that adage by saying, show me your friends and I will tell you where you are going, or what probably becomes of you in the nearest future." Personally, I remember very well that I had been exposed to sexually related activities from age twelve (12) as a result of the kind of friends that I related to and associated with. If you relate with smart and intelligent group, you will soon become one of them. Your life cannot be better than the people you surround yourself with. You have a role to play when it comes to selecting who you associate with, or whoever comes near you.

The kind of friends you keep will go a long way in determining how you achieve your dreams; how you make decisions about certain things in life; your appearance, those places you visit, what you eat and drink, and many more. Therefore, select your friends and those you will relate with outside your family with good care because they affect your life directly.

CHAPTER FIVE

TEENAGE PREGNANCY

Teenage pregnancy is often related to females below the age of eighteen having pregnancies which were unplanned for. This means that any pregnancy that occurs between the ages of thirteen and eighteen can be said to be teenage pregnancy. Any age younger than what I mentioned above is even worse. We have seen and heard more terrible stories of girls getting pregnant before they become teenagers in different parts of the world. It is rather sickening to know that some governments and communities around the world allow such practice even in this present time and season. Normally, an eighteen-year-old can be approved to be fully fit to be a mother under some circumstances, but not always advisable

In both developed and developing countries, teenage pregnancies are often associated with social issues, including lower educational levels, higher rates of poverty, and other poorer life outcomes. A lot of time, lack of exposure and education are a bigger factor why there is a high rate of teenage pregnancy. Whenever we talk about teenage pregnancy, we usually refer to the pregnancy of youths at an early stage of life that is unplanned and is outside marriage. Teenage pregnancy carries a social stigma in many communities and cultures with subjects unable to cope with the trauma.

By contrast, teenage parents in some countries may even be married, and their pregnancies welcomed by families and society. However, in such societies, even though they ascribe such practice to culture, they could also be faced with health challenges, birth complications, among other medical problems.

CAUSES OF TEENAGE PREGNANCY

Teenage pregnancy has become a growing concern nowadays and has, therefore, become imperative to look into the various causes of teenage pregnancy in order to deal with this subject matter carefully.

Teenage pregnancies are widely discouraged because the of health risks they raise for the young mothers including their babies. The list could be endless but, in this book, I carefully touched on some causes of teenage pregnancy which I believe will help in addressing the subject matter much better. It will also be good if take down some notes as you look at these causes critically so that you can tell which one really confronts you.

Among the major causes of teenage pregnancies are; having early sex among teenagers, lack of adequate sex education, lack of awareness about the causes and effects of teenage pregnancy more often than not, lack of proper communication between teenagers and their parents are said to be the major causes of unwanted teenage pregnancy. Therefore, it is the duty of parents to impart adequate knowledge about sex including reproductive health. This is very important because parents should normally be the first point of call for children and teenagers. The closer your parents are to you, the more things you want to share with them both consciously and unconsciously.

Social media also plays a negative role thereby making teenagers/youths vulnerable to early sex and as a result, become pregnant. And of course, because the teens in question do not have proper sex education, they are forced into committing abortions as they ultimately realize their inability to face the music or consequences that follow. Psychological factors such as having peer pressures as a result of the transition to puberty usually make some teenagers become irresponsible. Although, this is indicated in their lack of discipline and emotional control meaning that whenever there is a lack of discipline, factors like the use of alcohol and hard drugs accompanied by unrestricted interaction with the opposite sex can ignite lust and unnecessary passion ultimately leading to teenage pregnancy. An abuse of teenagers especially the girls could also be one of the causes of teenage pregnancy. Studies have shown that older men who derive pleasure in engaging teenage girls sexually will most likely lead to pregnancy than two teenagers dating one another. Also, strong family ties usually provide adequate emotional support for the teenagers in times of need.

When this emotional support is there, and is tested and trusted, there is nothing teenagers cannot tell you tend there will never be any reason to look elsewhere where they might be counselled wrongly.

I have been a teenage teacher for many years, and I can tell you over and over that 95% of the time, teenagers are always looking for love and trust and will naturally give to whoever offers them.

Moreover, parents who tend to show care always end up putting too many restrictions on their children, especially girls just because they want to protect them from dangers. Being aggressively overprotective can be dangerous for the child. There must be a balance between showing love and being overprotective.

From research, it has been discovered that this overprotection usually gives rise to frustration and a feeling of not being loved and cared for. Again, a measurable balance is important to avoid this kind of problem.

ADVERSE RESULTS OF TEENAGE PREGNANCY

Teenage pregnancies can create a host of other problems in which time and space may not allow for all to be listed here. However, some of them may be incomplete education which may mean dropping out of school early, unemployment, depression, poverty, social embarrassment, among a number of other emotional traumas, are some of the problems that can be created.

Furthermore, early motherhood also affects the psychological development of the child adversely. This is true because the bodies of teenage girls are not as developed as those of adult women in terms of childbearing; therefore, they are likely to face certain complications in the process of child delivery which can lead to maternal death most of the time. For the purpose of having a well-detailed explanation, here are some of the adverse effects as a result of teenage pregnancy. There is no way I would have been able to explain everything in detail, but few pieces here and there will add the adequate value to you as you read.

Medical Complications

Medical complications often occur in pregnant teenagers which usually require a lot of attention. According to the American Academy of Child and Adolescent Psychiatry (AACAP); too often, teenagers do not seek adequate medical care during the pregnancy thereby leading to complications. Different health challenges that normally occur could be high blood pressure, premature delivery of baby, Vesicovaginal Fistula -VVF (abnormal fistulous), placenta previa among others. Therefore, should a teenager become pregnant suddenly, it is important for ongoing medical care to be in place in order to prevent these complications from threatening the pregnancy and the mother's well-being.

Worries about Future

Uncertainty about the future may arise when there is an early pregnancy. The subject may feel they do not have enough knowledge to be a mother or a father at such an early stage. The Subject may also have fears about how having a baby will impact their lives and dreams for the future. No doubt, this state of worry can lead to depression. Depression might set in for a teenager who tries to manage the emotions and pressure from friends and acquaintances. Besides, the fluctuating hormones that pregnancy causes may also prompt depression. Depression is not good for both the child and the mother, and even the father.

Delayed Education

Education may be put on hold when a teen becomes pregnant or can lead to dropping out of school totally. The hopes and dreams of pursuing further studies at the college or university might be shattered as a result of early pregnancy. A major reason is that they may decide to focus on the baby for a while or sometimes even decide to get married rather than pursuing further education. Two things will definitely happen, its either you end your academic career abruptly or experience a delay. It is not a thing not to expect; because your attention will shift to a battle of survival of yourself and that of your baby.

Emotional Crisis

It is one thing to get pregnant as a child, it is another thing to keep the baby after birth.

Different emotional crisis such as confusion, resentment, sadness, anger, frustration, regrets, and may be experienced that might lead to rash behaviors such as wanting to kill the baby or commit suicide.

I remember some moments I was able to ask questions from some teenagers who got pregnant. I wanted to know the first emotional crisis they had to deal with when they first found out that they were pregnant. The answers were similar and one of the first crises they faced was how to talk to their parents, the father of the baby including his parents. At this stage, few of them said they felt they had betrayed their loved ones, and some felt like taking their own lives, abscond or even drop out of school. The regrets and shame were just too much to bear.

There are many choices in pregnancy that she will need to face such as ending the pregnancy, giving it up for adoption, or keeping the baby.

The emotional trauma and negative thoughts interfere with so many activities, academics, and social well-being of teenagers. All of these do happen due to the fear of the unknown.

Exhaustion

One typical advice that I will in addition to what your medical experts might tell you is to take enough rest as much as possible. If you are reading this book at this time and you find yourself in this situation of having to deal with an unwanted, and other teenage pregnancy challenges, please note that exhaustion may arise, as it is normal during this period but just relax, it is not the end of the world my friend. You can still become whatever dreams and vision you set for yourself. You and the baby are the most important thing right now and keep trusting that you will come out of this stronger.

Loneliness

Many teenage mothers find that when they tell the father of the baby about the pregnancy, they break up immediately and the lady is now left to deal with the situation all alone. And even after the break-up, things may still not go the same way it used to be. In most advanced countries around the world, the father is supposed to pay for child support in cases like this; but this rarely happens because most times, the father himself is rather poor and totally dependent on the parents. So, the teenage expecting mother will have to bear the burdens all by herself. Sometimes, teenagers will suffer some physical effects which could make them keep to themselves. Sometimes, studies revealed they are depressed and at some point, might have considered suicide as an option.

Neglect of Baby

Once the baby is born, teenagers may not be willing or able to give desired attention to their babies' needs. A teen may not be an adequate mother because she is already overwhelmed by the constant needs and attention the baby seeks. She may grow annoyed at the lack of freedom to interact with her peer group due to the baby's needs. Neglect may also be from the father who may never show up or give any form of assistance or support.

Financial Trouble

Financial difficulty may arise during a teen pregnancy or even after the baby is born. Imagine a situation whereby you are still under your parents and solely depend on them to meet your needs. If you cannot comfortably take care of yourself, how then would you be able to raise a baby who now totally depends on you? Teens who do not have full-time employment or who their parents are not wealthy may struggle to cover the basic expenses of life upon having a baby.

Abortion or murder

This route to end a pregnancy has psychological and emotional consequences some more intense depending on the belief system. While some teenagers may consider abortions, some will decide in their hearts to kill the baby as soon as they have them. I have heard a few times of cases where people (youths most especially) throw their babies in the toilet. The last one I heard was terrifying because the baby was found in the toilet pipe. It's traumatic what you may want to try once you discover that you are pregnant at a very early stage of your life.

The best approach to avoid these traumas is to abstain from sex at a very early stage when you know you cannot dare the consequences that will follow.

Time as a grown adult comes when you will be very free to have sex any time and anyhow you like with your lovely partner without anyone questioning or anything stopping you.

So, I tell you to wait until that time.

Moreover, there are some physical risks attached to forced abortions especially at a very young age. Risks such as:

> ➢ Allergic reaction
> ➢ Blood clots
> ➢ Incomplete abortion
> ➢ Infection
> ➢ Injury to cervix or other organs
> ➢ Undetected ectopic pregnancy
> ➢ Heavy bleeding that could sometimes lead to death

CHAPTER SIX

PARENTAL AND TEACHERS' GUIDE

One of the most important things for all parents to note is that the issue of sex and everything that relates to it is not supposed to be avoided or ignored, but to approach it head-on so that children can learn about sex and relationships with others (especially the opposite sex) from their most trusted source which is you.

In your home, placing a complete ban on the use of social media is almost unrealistic nowadays. Somehow, the kids know how to outsmart you the parent, accessing different contents to their satisfaction. You will be amazed to know that an average teenager devotes close to seven hours surfing the internet out of 24 hours daily. You will be amazed to know that 33% of online contents contain sexual images or porn references.

Therefore, here are a few ways to ensure that children and teens are tutored and nurtured in the right direction to avoid early exposure.

Know what your children watch, play, and listen to and take advantage of teachable moments to discuss any inappropriate content or behaviors with them. Parental guidance is key to living in this present jet-age filled with so many distractions.

Set and enforce limits around screen time. Your children must be taught to be disciplined by themselves such that whether you are present with them or not, they do not go outside the privilege.

Make use of Internet filters, passwords, and other useful parental controls. Unfortunately, many parents all over the world must know how they can place restrictions on what their children have access to online. However, this trend is changing as many parents are getting informed daily on this.

Share your family's values and expectations regarding sex and relationships with your children often at a very early stage of their lives. Let them know how you will feel if things go the other way around.

Most times, children will refuse to do a thing that will endanger them especially when they know that it will not only affect them but everyone around them as well.

Talk to your child about social media representations of sex, relationships, and gender roles and teach them to question the accuracy and intent of the messages they receive from all platforms.

Model healthy, respectful relationships and self-worth and do not hesitate to reward their good and right decisions when they share their encounters with you.

I wish you all the best life has to offer, even as you use, all the good virtues you have learned through this book.

Share with others what you learned.

Personal Notes

Personal Notes